In the Lily Room

In the Lily Room

Erica Hesketh

Nine
Arches
Press

In the Lily Room
Erica Hesketh

ISBN: 978-1-916760-16-5
eISBN: 978-1-916760-17-2

First published May 2025 by:

Nine Arches Press
Studio 221, Zellig
Gibb Street, Deritend
Birmingham
B9 4AU
United Kingdom

www.ninearchespress.com

Printed on recycled paper in the United Kingdom by:
Imprint Digital.

Nine Arches Press is supported using public funding by:
Arts Council England.

Supported using public funding by
ARTS COUNCIL ENGLAND

Contents

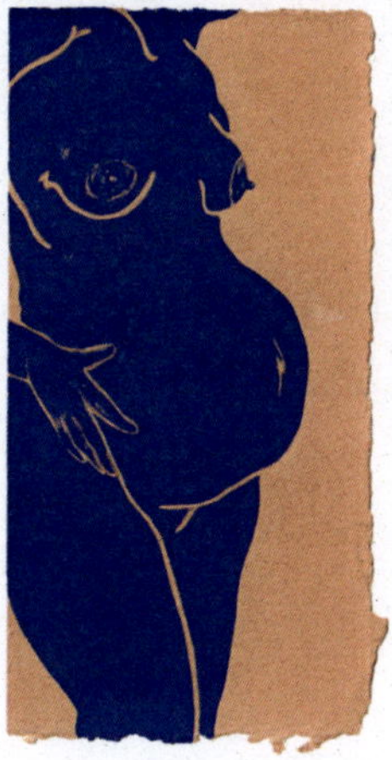

Tidings

the person is stretching their legs in their sleep

they say: *comfort and half-light*
I do not know if it is a question or a command

they say: *the tide, the bone palace, my heart*

and I am in the crimped air of the ultrasound clinic
ah yes, there is the vulva, he says

she says: *give me plums, give me figs, take that smell away*

if I sit far enough away from the fridge
if I sing songs that make me cry on the sofa
child of mine, child of mine

she says: *what will I find at the far reaches of this room*
unfolding like a paper fan

if I lose my temper on the plane
if I slump down in the corner of the restaurant

she says: *I am interested, show me something*
and I take her to a foaming river

and the sound is a billion, billion bubbles

she says: *sheep's wool and crunchy petals*
I do not know if it is a wish or a complaint

she says: *shall we go and shake a tree*

and I am ringed by curtains in the triage bay

I say: love, I don't think I can do this
what if everything that follows is loss

if you are a stranger
if I have fooled myself

she says: *mother, mother*
we're ready for you, they say

Birth notes

Time without season.
A hand in a rushing stream.
Begin anywhere.

A sow hunches on a bed.
A queen shouts out from her throne.

A day in triage,
watching clouds gently collide
from a high window.

I wait for you to return
with sweets and massage oil.

Start of a new shift.
The moon must be on her way.
A sphere of our own.

A brisk Trinidadian
nurse at the foot of the bed.

In her mother's house
a bowl of ripening mango
and carambola.

Sprays of bright chaconia
hanging heavy in the yard.

One centimetre.
You're on your way now, she says,
taking off her glove.

I grip your hand, picturing
the colour-coded wall chart.

Six pink-cheeked women
sweating in cotton dresses,
taking careful notes.

> *On a scale of one to ten,*
> *how confident do you feel?*

Cicada hissing
from an orange classroom chair,
evangelical.

> 'Accelerated labour'.
> Four minutes from crest to crest.

The first contraction
stretches like a lake towards
a ball bearing moon.

> Her orbit will grow tighter.
> Time reversing on water.

Time-lapse peony
opening its thick petals,
crushing them again.

> The day's light vanishes in
> thirty-second rotations.

A syrupy dark.
We do not turn on a lamp
or ring a phone-in.

> Forty seconds now… fifty…
> A doctor walks in, walks out.

A midwife called Grace
arrives to administer
antibiotics.

The screams of other women
leap between open windows.

My gentle husband
pushing my back to bruising,
as hard as you can…

The page of my mind is full
of pictures that can't be right.

Eels in the car park.
A fox in hospital scrubs
chewing the linens.

Emergency C-sections
bleating down the corridor.

Fully dilated.
I tell you to stop counting
and run for your life.

Everything washes away –
cities, rivers, continents –

Beautiful moon :
show your face through this fearsome
tempest! Pity me –

On two knees, baring my teeth,
fingers white on the bedpost –

I can see her head,
Grace whispers into the gloom –
Your eyes are on me –

Rising now, above the room –
Whatever else happens, love –

We stood together
on the early morning bus,
lashes wet with dew –

A cloudburst and she is here.
Whatever else happens, love.

Tree frog in my lap,
wet limbs folded, preparing
to draw first breath…

A slick coating of vernix.
Snow melting before a frost.

Placenta

in the beginning, spiral arteries unwound

a river thundered to the site
where the capsule was buried,
flesh into flesh, bathing the villi in blood:
our first exchange

within days a structure
sprang up along the outermost wall,
a trading post that would balloon
into a roaring bazaar

teeming with vessels from both sides
bearing bottled air, fresh supplies,
faecal waste, heady hormone clouds,
white flags of phosphocholine –

everything you need to build a world,
and all without a single drop of blood
tumbling over the border

stand back

to marvel at the bright metropolis,
fairy tale of eternal growth,
where futures were traded
behind chemical shields

electricity! jazz! foreigners! excess!
arteries at capacity and everyone you met
only ever passing through

to fall in love in such a place,
blood deafening, fingers plunged
into the very same well of history,
never quite touching

nine months from cyst to city,
cradle of civilisation making ready
to launch a human into space

that day the sea drained dry,
the sky collapsed in red clumps
but the tether held, quietly shipping
the last of the oxygen

then you peeled away from the uterine wall,
followed your charge into the cold,
slipped into the waiting bucket
and were gone

Indications

There was the sound of pumps going.
Sticky heat. An always-light.

Time was strange,
weighed in sensations, the changing

of shifts, of sanitary towels,
the smell of food nearly ready.

We took it on trust,
we didn't speak the language.

After a while a nurse
would come, a sales rep, someone

with an unfilled form and pen.
We held out our hands.

A sudden blast of sound
when a larger family swept in

with all the outside world
clinging to their coats.

At eleven and two the feeding
video would start up again

in the room with the air-conditioning,
white sky from the window.

The women who were delivered
padded about in bare feet.

Some cried silently.
Some were elated all of the time.

There wasn't space
to be unsure.

Latch

In the postnatal ward there was
an artist, with bird's-nest hair.

Every morning she would wheel
her baby in its plastic cot

to the coffee urn and say
hello, in a small grey voice.

In another life I think
we might have been friends.

Every afternoon I would see her
in the breastfeeding room

at the end of the hall, trying and trying
to get her baby to latch.

Her nipples were like two black eyes
but she wouldn't give up, she

needed this one thing.

I think about her every time
someone tells me that

of course
breastfeeding is a choice.

How she was beautiful, the way
rain clouds are often beautiful.

Breast is best. It's up to you to choose, mummy.
If you switch now the child will be confused, mummy.

The only thing that only I can do and I'm failing.
You must present the breast on baby's cues, mummy.

Between attempts, my thumbs try to coax the milk—
Press too hard and you'll leave another bruise, mummy.

The doctor said she's lost too much weight. Could formula—
We told you from the start it's up to you, mummy.

Could you just give us some space to figure—
You're fine, mummy. It's only baby blues, mummy.

Pupae

Behind mauve curtains
clinked all the way shut along a curved rail

we broke down
our larval structures

each of us held fast to a thin white sheet
our safe leaf

by a button of silk
we made ourselves

before yesterday's shell gave way
to this baffling gold.

Four dolls to a bay we wait
for damp wings to punch

fully formed
through chiffon skin.

A handsome couple

The living room walls
were too quiet
after the clamouring of the ward
so we fled uphill

to a bench in the breeze,
delirious escapees with
no inkling we had
brought the prison with us.

The shock of vinegar
from the parted chip paper,
crushed batter releasing
plumes of new steam.

We could still
just about see our former life.
This isn't too bad,
we said to one another.

Dusk fell.
Muddling the pram
around potholes we saw
a handsome couple approaching

on the far pavement.
Her hands at rest,
light jumper stretched
across a full-term belly.

Oh, we gaped
from the other side
of the membrane.

Pigeon

When the lift opened onto the fourth floor (Babies & Children), the dread was already there. It draped over us like a shroud and our noses filled with camphor, the memory of damp churches. We had come to find the cot we'd need in half a year's time, though it was clear this was a timeframe we could not possibly comprehend. We shuffled out of the lift with our faces on. Uncountable cotton sleepsuits wobbled headless on their hangers either side of an eternal polished walkway, which slid under our feet and refused to lead to the Lebanese pop-up indicated on the floor plan. A stranger padded past, cradling a tiny pair of shoes which held my gaze for longer than was comfortable. It was at this point that the pigeons burst from my mother's mouth, like furred tennis balls from a tennis ball machine. They began to race around at head height, shitting on the toys that beeped, dropping greasy black feathers onto wingback nursing chairs that no one could afford. I needed to sit down; the café appeared like a page-turn. The teacups were decorated with a mosaic of tiny blue and white teeth. I was impossibly tired. Why did everything have to remind me of death… When I looked up the pram was gone. I turned to my husband saying 'where is—' but just then one of the pigeons flew into my mouth and became lodged in my throat. I could feel its feather shafts snapping as we struggled against one another, both trying to get free.

Diagnosis

back again on the hard blue chair
a month-old baby as my ballast

knowing this time we will all drown
except it's only me who's underwater

Female Immersed

might get people talking
if it were a sheep or tiger shark

but this piece has been done to death
one in ten mothers

The Physical Impossibility of
Reaching the Tissues on the Desk

please, I say, polite, toes pressing the lino

(suffer enough that they take you seriously
not so much that they take her away)

please stop telling me how articulate I am
and do something   I can't

breathe in here

Postpartum

In another world, I'm sure I laced my tea with fenugreek.
Yes, I dressed my front door with garlands of straw and pine
and lay in state for five days, while a young woman
from the village rubbed salt into my swollen feet.
In another world, I know I rested for the full thirty days.
I avoided hot baths. Or I avoided cold baths. My hair lay
tangled on the pillow like a serpent's shed skin. I saw it.
In another world, I shied away from men, shielded them
from my unholy body, the uncertainty slipping
like scarlet silverfish down my thighs. My sheets were
buried quickly under the floorboards. In another world,
the colostrum dried out in my breasts. Or I nursed freely,
day and night, day and night, never offending any ghosts.
In another world, I packed my bags and returned
to my mother's house, to be fed, washed, taught what
a mother was, at last, to be grateful. In another world,
I must have been surrounded for a hundred nights by wild,
wise, luminous women who stroked my cheeks and wept
for the beautiful things I had lost. In another world,
I may have slept for forty days while those exact women
mixed elixirs from angelica root, honey, cracked seaweed,
their heavy plaits thudding like boots on their backs.
The questions drying out in my mouth. What is. Why did. Would it have.
In another world, other hands may have soothed my baby
while I watched from under a thick blanket. Maybe I ate
nothing but hot foods to counteract my feminine nature,
so spongy and unfinished. In another world, they may have
hoisted me above an open fire and left me to sweat it out.
To cure. To counteract. We have no way of knowing.

To the concerned spouse

Japanese creation myth

Motherhood has killed her and she has left you for the land of the dead. Of course you wish to see her so you have followed, bravely, on foot, but when you arrive she tells you she has already eaten a meal cooked in the ovens of the underworld, and therefore can never return to you. Try not to lose your patience. Do not hold a torch to her face while she is sleeping – you will realise she has become a rotting corpse. If you betray her like this she will send forth hags of thunder and hordes of screaming warriors to chase you from the land of the dead. You may try to distract them by tossing out the vines which secure your hair, your finely crafted comb. These will transform mid-air into grapes and bamboo shoots, to be devoured by the hordes. You may try to pelt the hags with sweet, fragrant peaches which grow abundantly along the path back to the land of the living. Whatever you do, do not try to block the path with a boulder; this will only cause her to pronounce a curse on all creation, wiping out one thousand mortals each day, and if she does that you will have to beget one thousand five hundred mortals each day, just to keep up.

Voice Note to self

I couldn't help but notice
how good you look in those dungarees,
how serenely you crossed over
the platform just now, still feeding,
one hand firm across your baby's back
like you've been doing this
for years and not four shaky weeks –
I couldn't help but notice
how your lopsided breasts tell a story,
the beauty of your whole body
stepping into the shower
at strange times of day,
how meticulously you plan
in order to have the space to be
the responsive mother you wanted –
I couldn't help but notice
your determination
to make this relationship work,
the way you talk about mothering
as work, how frank you are
without ever thinking it brave,
the solace that gives –
I couldn't help but notice
how ravaged you are and yet
how utterly engrossed,
the way she looks at you,
the way she looks just like you,
how miraculously –

Water music

On Tuesdays mornings we gathered | at the community centre

like rivers at the valley floor | heavy with sediment

one by one | one by one

finding a chair in the circle | our babies like reed baskets at our feet

You might think there was music | and in a way there was

That great ocean rumble | before the baton lifts

—

When we were ready | the first person would begin

I'm terrified of hurting her | Is it wrong that I'm so bored

line by line | line by line

speaking the week | while the rest of us nodded and sighed

like grasses along the sand banks | of our childhoods

You might think there was music | and in a way there was

—

For half a year we | wove ourselves together

Where did my life go | When will I love my body again

row by row | row by row

shapes that would hold | for a week or more this time

while at our feet our moons | waxed and waxed

and in our chests | that deep-boned waltz

—

Once the babies were crawling | we would need to leave

We watched them like spiders | as they watched our mouths

week by week | week by week

pushing out the words | confessing to one another

that this was still as much | world as we could handle

You might think there was music | and in a way there was

Compline

The Lord Almighty grant us a quiet night.
The Lord Almighty grant us six quiet hours.
The Lord Almighty grant us two quiet hours.
The Lord Almighty grant us one hour.

The Lord Almighty grant us a quick feed.
The Lord Almighty grant us a comfortable chair.
The Lord Almighty grant us a packet of biscuits within reach.
The Lord Almighty grant us a glass of water within reach.

The Lord Almighty grant us a good latch and a friend on WhatsApp.
The Lord Almighty grant us a good latch.
The Lord Almighty grant us an imperfect latch.
The Lord Almighty grant us consolation.

The Lord Almighty grant us a clear cobalt sky.
The Lord Almighty grant us clouds that gambol in the moonlight.
The Lord Almighty grant us moonlight.
The Lord Almighty grant us a darkness
    that envelops but does not suffocate.

Kintsugi

Mother of the deep – underwater mother
draped in weeds, pushing your way across the sea bed,
green lips releasing breath as rosary beads:
you will get through today.

Mother of stone – petrified mother
perched on the cliff face, menaced by raptors,
fluttering petitions, the impossible monuments:
you will get through today.

Mother of ice – translucent mother
floating among the warm flamingo bodies, mouth
shut tight to keep the chill from spreading:
you will get through today.

Mother of small beasts – quivering mother
with ears pressed back, alert to every faint
threat or slight, rattling your hollow quills:
you will get through today.

Mother of the dark – moonstruck mother
locked in a strange orbit, tidal milk rising
and still rising under your eerie surface:
you will get through today.

Mother of mulch – mouldering mother
weighed down by the silence of the forest,
spores of doubt plotting paths beneath the soil:
you will get through today.

Mother of fire – righteous mother laying waste
to everything in the master's house, host to a rage
that thrills you even as it boils your blood:
you will get through today.

Mother of sand – scattered mother losing time
in clumps, your self in drifts, ashamed
in your bewilderment: you will,
you will get through today.

Know that you are magnificent because
you bear the marks of your transformation.
Mother of clay – gold-veined mother:
you will get through today.

In praise of Sertraline

Day five and the sun finally rises without effort.
By mid-morning it is alert at its desk, anglepoise beam
loosening the small green shoots in the meadow

where dog walkers are shooting the breeze,
a trio of tin-cloth coats wrapped in momentum.

From this hillcrest I am noticing the radiance
of everything that grows – cow parsley and phlox,
plump maple leaves, the skin of your face as you sleep –

and wondering if the devastating beauty of youth
is nothing more, or less, than cell division.

Thoughts like cirrus clouds; the smell of cut grass.
I am quite still and today, at least, that is all right.
A breath escapes and I remember the day

teenage me first saw individual leaves on a tree,
outside an optician's on the other side of the world,

how it transformed in an instant from what
I had been taught it was – an overripe symbol,
a blur along the road – into the thing itself.

Night feed

Daughter attempting to fall asleep on the breast:
I cherish you as you study the problem

from every angle, hot-cheeked locksmith
carefully coaxing pin after pin,

picking the combination with your whole mouth.
One day you will tip into orgasm

with this same quiet focus. Don't ever change.
Tell your lover, or whoever, exactly

what it is you want – their hair out of the way,
the weight of their warm hands just so.

South London air

The truth is you can't see yourself living anywhere else.
NO_x You like knowing you can hop a few stops,
shoulder to shoulder with the world, and be *right there*
on the red carpet, at the heart CO_2 of a private view,
in amongst it with the hipsters, the writers, the punch
SO_x of Turkish coffee, bibimbap, sliders, udon, jerk, sizzling
flat irons behind CH_4 French windows, revolution! –
or you could, once she starts sleeping through.

To be a Londoner means participating NO_x
in the life everyone else sees on TV: that could be you,
CFC queuing for The Tennis; queuing for The Sale;
raising your placard high NO_x outside the actual Houses of Parliament;
adding your SO_x histories to the fat snake of the Thames
CO_2 as the EastEnders credits roll; finding your tribe…

You could still find your tribe. She will, CH_4 you're sure of it.

For now CO_2 you're learning to keep your breaths shallow.
You're learning SO_x what it is to weather CFC each day,
how to angle her away CH_4 from the traffic when it's a long wait
SO_x for a bus and sometimes when NO_x a few NO_x in a row NO_x
thunder past already CH_4 clogged up with CO_2 other buggies
you're learning SO_x to cut your NO_x losses CH_4 and walk.

On a clear day from the top of Blythe Hill, though –
the wind whistling towards all that steel and glass –

Abecedary

At baby yoga, Aidan's mummy is describing her prolapse. Betty's mummy had one too, with her first, so she didn't take any chances this time around.

At the breastfeeding hub, Caitlin's mummy says she was terrified of doing her first poo, kept it in for a fortnight. 'There's a lot they don't warn you about,' says Danny's mummy at the bus stop, with an angry laugh.

'I've been wearing a giant nappy for a month,' says Evie's mummy at the weigh-in. At the stay-and-play, Florence's mummy asks if anyone else's hair is falling out, and everyone reaches up to touch their own heads.

George's mummy says she lost so much blood she couldn't grip a pen for three weeks, in the queue at Asda. At the library sing-along, Harriet and Isla's mummy jokes about the doctors pouncing on her in the delivery room, the way they barked at her from every direction under a merciless light.

Jules's mummy has been decanting formula into a Medela bottle because she can't admit she's given up feeding. In the garden centre, Kai's mummy realises she doesn't want anything more to do with other mummies.

Leon's mummy and Mina's mummy jog around the park with their ergonomic prams, comparing mastitis symptoms. Naomi's mummy really wanted to join them today, is screaming at her partner for not waking her in time.

Oscar's mummy still messages the mums group during night feeds but the replies have stopped coming. Priya's mummy has turned off her notifications because everyone else's life looks so rosy.

At the swimming pool, Queenie's mummy thinks the midwives may have stitched her up too tight. At Mindful Mums, Reggie's mummy uses the word *resentment*. Saskia's mummy thinks everything is colic, or teeth. Her hands flutter around her face.

On a park bench Theo's mummy asks Una's mummy if she can stay at hers for a bit, just until she can sort out somewhere more permanent.

Vita's mummy hasn't gone out since the delivery – she's waiting for the shadows to stop stalking her bedroom. William's mummy and Xavier's mummy have sacked off baby sensory and are in the pub at opening time.

'I never realised how much I'd need my own mother,' says Yolanda's mummy, at the airport.

Zora's mummy pounds the pavement, while Zora dreams.

How horribly fast a name so soft, so wanted,
can grow rough with overuse: mummy.

I used to know precisely who I was, but I don't
recognise this drifting, diffuse 'mummy'.

Some things are true. The way she rests her hand on—
A matter for the developmental reviews, mummy.

I don't want to use this pump at work, the sound alone is—
Beginning of the end if you refuse, mummy.

Preparation

breast milk how to store nhs
breast milk freezer bags reusable

She never complained, not even once,
diligently pumping after each feed.

Seven months (we all knew the deadline)
to fill her freezer with carefully labelled storage bags

– sourced online for their superior capacity,
and ability to lie completely flat –

ahead of the big day.
The duty of the working mother

would be to provide in absentia and in advance,
to have already thought of everything;

she knew this like she knew the weight
of the infant on her chest,

the perfect weight of his sleeping head
against the palm of her hand,

all that she was giving up
by reclaiming the mantle of herself.

We had a power cut last week, she said,
lightly shouldering this, too.

Safety advice

Always lay her flat on her back, feet aligned
with the foot of the cot. Remember
woollen blankets can be a choking hazard.
Keep her close to you at all times. Use your hand
to support the back of her neck. Remember
a baby can drown in an inch of water.
Keep medicines and sharp kitchen utensils
out of reach, out of sight. Scan the sky
when you leave any building. Remember
low-flying aircraft may not trigger the sirens.
Keep a suitcase packed. Memorise the locations
of your nearest shelters. Make sure the last
names on your personal documents match
to avoid being separated at the border.
Consider preparing Molotov cocktails.
Write the word CHILD on a piece of paper
and tape it to the back window of your car.
Write the word CHILDREN in white paint
on the pavement outside the theatre –
as big as you can, this is important –
before you go belowground.

Ball python wife

It's happening again
    I can feel the keratin

click-clicking from my fingertips
over the backs of my hands

braceleting my wrists
advancing on the poor yellow

flesh of my elbows   a smother
of pearlescent plates

what will happen to me
when this reaches my pits

my throat   already my eyes
are lidless and milky

my jaw is aching
from its slow stretch

my legs   blotched and brown
have begun to fuse

from the groin
    the air tastes very cold

I want to tell you I am scared
but my tongue has split open

so I curl up
against your back

    a lacquered fist

Horniman Gardens, December

The oaks are shrouded in mist,
    a lake of frozen bodies
        lit by a falling, cosmic dust.

Today the cold clings like death.
    Thin canvas shoes crunch, too loud
        on the frosted path.

The sheep exhale at the gate,
    anxious for the four o'clock bell.
        One more hour of milky light.

One more loop around the meadow.
    One more push up the promenade
        made beastly by shadows.

The chill bones of a mother
    slotting into place, pushing off,
        one after the other.

Suddenly a robin's cry
    takes shape, too close,
        an unbidden memory.

And you keep walking, waiting
    for the warden's bell to toll *home,*
        home, a hex lifting.

And peace to men on earth

O little no of nerve-endings,
how full we signs of teeth.
Away the day and dreamless thought
intrusive tinselled wreath;
yet in this marriage sleeping
persistent clanging weight.
The paper strewn of love-worn years
are sodden sky tonight.

Precociousness of merry
and babbled sippy cold
while mortals tile the Sertraline
their strips of tepid pool.
O glitter bauble family
in secret overcast,
then bright eyes sing to ravaged was
and weeks to later first.

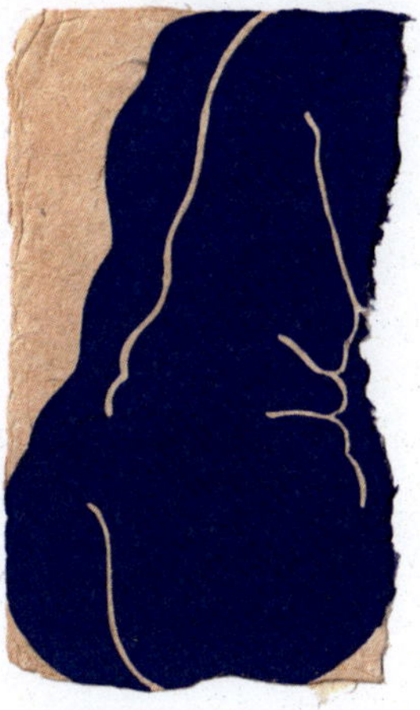

Scenes from our bed

1.

Fresh peach; we worship
her nose as it lifts to meet
our pinching fingers.

2.

The rumbling trains.
Our slumbering neighbourhood
underneath a mackerel sky.

3.

My mind is racing.
What if all the world's mothers
rose up at once…

4.

White narcissus;
at night we scroll through pictures
on our phones and weep.

5.

Rain on our window.
Rain on our baby's window
through the monitor.

6.

Waking from a dream.
A flock of bright kingfishers
in a sleeping bag.

The fish

My mother sent an iron fish
from Kanagawa for my anaemia.
It arrived in a small, grey box
with exclamation marks
all over it – *WE PRESENT FOR YOU!!*
HEALTHY LIFE!! – and a cartoon
of a similar fish across the lid,
though that one seemed angry,
with spiked fins and heavy eyebrows,
whereas the fish waiting inside
bore no expression at all.
I held her in my dry palm
– in those days everything
which had the power to alter me
was female – but couldn't decide
whether she was heavier
or lighter than I had expected.
Her body was coin-coloured,
the colour of damp roofs,
her scales like little plates arranged
in an overlapping pattern, neat
and round as if drawn on
by a studious child. Through a hole
in her soft metal mouth
was a plain white string
tied in a loop, a toy seaside
donkey's lead, or an austere belt
for a tiny Buddhist monk.
I lowered her into a saucepan
halfway full with water,
turned on the gas.
I watched as the water

did nothing at first and then
began to tremble, noting
with a lone lit corner of my mind
the bubbles forming
like a shawl of tiny pearls
across her back.
The fish stayed very still,
offering no resistance
as the metallic taste of her
small, hard body
mingled imperceptibly
with the warming water.
As the day got going outside
I stood in the shadow
of the kitchen door,
fingers wrapped weakly
around my empty cup, thinking
it wouldn't be so bad
to curl up inside another woman's
womb for a while. Then
the water reached its limit
and big, gulping air pockets
rushed suddenly to the surface
like pearl divers in Toba Bay –
naked, radiant, beautiful, free –
and I lost sight of her.

The body remembers

this focus inwards – hands still
busy with the nappy, mouth blowing soft raspberries

the sloughing off, the monthly slaughter

stepping quickly to the toilet before
fat slugs – beet, blackberry, rust – overwhelm

the pitiful cotton strip

though not if it would mean
leaving the baby unattended, even for a minute

keeping your breaths calm and slow

bleeding down your legs
while you start the lullaby again, holding a fretful hand

soap and cold water at the kitchen sink

thousands of you in the bleak night
poring over the entrails

the strange relief

being too young and then – later –
being relieved when you weren't supposed to be

there is a reason you keep your mouth shut

but the body remembers
that early autumn morning

red cloud in the bowl

never wanting anything more in your whole useless life
brow pressed against cold tile

That summer

—our melodrama was the ocean. We were heartsick in anticipation, our looks full-laden with meaning. We stumbled about with eyes like blown bulbs, jealousy giving way to bliss, hope morphing into a yowling fear of death. We resented the future. We marvelled at oaks. We hated pollution. We worshipped the sound of our voices laughing together, their mirror cadence. We despised capitalism. We whispered *I don't want you to die,* holding hands on the pedestrian bridge and waving hello to the trains. We were lovers under a wide open window in Paris, sweltering in the knowledge of the heartless working week, its callous first train ready to pull the one away from the other like a startled cloth out from under a vase falling, the hateful kilometres hardening like poured concrete—

Why are you awake?

I saw her tumble
out of a high window
white as a moon plummeting
her limbs a swan

it happened so quickly
my eyes flew into the night
but all they found
was the afterimage repeating

Live action role-play

The astronomer puts away her charts, eyes hollow
from the night shift. The cow stands to empty her udders

while the sergeant pulls on her fatigues and walks through
the day's manoeuvres. Dawn spills across rooftops.

At the front door, the rickshaw driver and the kangaroo
flip a coin to see who gets the morning shift.

The café soon fills up with the usual cast: the Avon lady,
the snake-charmer, the stenographer with her head down.

The psychic has cocked up and packed the wrong
colour cup. The logistics supervisor throws up her hands but

the clown is already halfway into her trousers,
one hand juggling a dozen carnations.

Where the herbalist was sitting there is now
a four-poster bed. Solidarity, says the cow from her stall.

Afternoon rolls in and the caravan winds its way
to the park, realm of the botanist with bright eyes.

At the swings, the actor tries out scraps of stale script.
The diplomat considers how much to give away.

In a quiet corner the translator murmurs to her client
about bears, about hats which hide in plain sight.

The paramedic arrives to deal with a minor incident
while the folk musician leads all the cows and beds

in song. The PA glances at her watch and nudges
the photographer, who is cleaning her lens again.

In the liquid light of evening the lover spoons out
frothy nothings while the masseuse warms her hands.

The architect's new tower collapses, which calls for
a turn from the running man. I wonder sometimes

if the gamemasters are even watching, she says,
doing up her hi-tops. The cleaner laughs into her bucket.

Later the philosopher continues her blistering treatise
on the third shift, while the composer workshops

her chorale for massed female voices, the one
that is going to make the world weep.

The cow looks up at the night sky, wishing she could
read it, as the astronomer settles into her chair.

Sleep songs

I.

I am thinking back to when
you were a tiny mammal on my chest, and we
would walk around the Horniman gardens – I far too awake
and you drifting to sleep, splendid fingers curled up
like a coral polyp under the hull of my chin.
The newsreader in my headphones would tell me
the Brexit talks were going badly: each morning
both sides seemed to find new ways to fail.
We were grafted together that summer. Pressing
my lips to your fast-hardening skull I remember
feeling my heart shrivel with love,
though I know it was actually growing around you,
the way rootstock grows around a scion bud
when the cut has been well made…

II.

Heart as rootstock – heart as reef – I remember
the way your little maw latched on to my limestone body – the moon
observing us from a different dot on its axis each night,
the shimmer of distant city lights, dancing
high above the surface of those blue-green hours.
In the mornings the grief would be back.
The Amazon would be burning on the news again, treetops
overwhelmed by putrid smoke, the purple stain –
I would tie you to my trunk and start walking, begging
love to pull the goodness up through me,
gift you something better than this done-for planet.
You would look up at me from my chest
with the calm reassurance of a daytime moon,
nod off at the gate…

III.

The copper beech bloomed green, then titian orange.
I would stop under it, holding you awkwardly
like a bag of windfall apples, tilt my head right back
to watch its dazzling paper-cut patterns bounce against the light.
Winter arrived early, bringing news of fresh
protests in Hong Kong, floods in Venice, yet another
general election. In the gardens the gourds were plump
and the morning glory had finished for the year.
You were sitting up on your own by then; I was
taking each day and night as they came, trying to keep
my tumbledown mind from falling in on us both.
But oh, how I loved your face when you first saw snow –
like the sky had beckoned you to the window
to tell you its very best secret…

IV.

I still remember when
we brought you home in your basket, the awe
and the heartbreak of it. I would sit and wait for you to wake,
anxious for your tentacle fingers to reach up
and tell me you were ready to be held again.
Holding you now I can feel your muscle, strength
in the sapling legs which take you farther each morning.
Heart as rootstock – heart as reef – we spent
all those nights on the sofa, watching moonlight fish
chasing each other across the carpet.
Little coral, I will not forget that silvery time.
But oh, how I love being bright with you under the new blossom,
knowing you are growing straight
and will sleep soundly when I lay you in your bed…

I can do this. I still feel flattened. I can do this.
The knowledge is growing in my bones whose mummy

I am: this remarkable human, this limpid mirror, this—
Just wait till you hit the terrible twos, mummy.

Boat

There are days when it comes flooding back:
Mother laid out flat, allowing fat tears to run
sideways off her cheeks because the dark
had come despite everything, peripheral vision
filling with black lines, a cage of cloud, no way
to call out to the beautiful world.

There are days, still, when the world
rushes at her with such a force she staggers back
into the swell, the millions of ways
she will harm her baby taking turns to run
her through with bayonets. A hateful vision
she thought she'd buried in the dark:

Mother at the bottom of the well, alone-dark –
staring up at the full moon of the world,
panicked breath blurring her vision –
a humid shout rising and falling back
empty, heart pounding up the walls as if trying to run
as far away as it could and in a way

she was the gull caught in the oil spill and in a way
the oil spill too, crude spreading dark
across the water like shame across a towel. She would run
out of love and stall, exposed to the world
like a sailboat in a lull. *Come back* (or was it *get back*),
a tinny voice crying out from the television—

This is like scratching at a vision,
hopeless, the facts slipping away.
Did I really throw crude oil at your back?
I remember we hauled ourselves up in the dark
night after night, cut off from the world.
I remember you didn't run.

Fourteen months for the water to run
clear and still you waited, the life we had envisioned
stowed safe above the shoreline, while the world
swept between our heavy centres, the way
water moves between moons in the dark,
warmth between bodies lying back to back

—until the day the world whispered to her, *run*
up the sail, the wind is back. The hope in the vision:
Mother on her way, pulling ropes in the dark.

Tradition

And at the end of that day
we were sat together by your bed
when suddenly you said

Dadda –

two square syllables, new
and delightful in their clarity.
We all applauded.

I've just recalled it – the certainty
that we three would go on
celebrating each other

like this, that this
would be what our family did,
what it meant.

You know the feeling

your legs are lead
there's been no sleep to speak of in weeks
you're shrinking from the headwind like it's a beating
and when exactly did you become
someone who shrinks
and once again the bottom of the pram is
a mess   all right   *the very idea*
that you could have another   I swear to god

and then you see it
the 185

rounding the bend towards your stop
a clear hundred yards
three minutes early what the actual
and the blood begins to pump
through your sullen heart
fascinating   and you are

a lioness after the kill
the Delorean at a minute after ten
Super Saturday Ennis-Hill

well go on then!

pram skittering along the edge of the pavement
past the snaking queue at the pharmacy
the vacated nail bars   *go!*
the shuttered Chinese takeaway
weaving with ease around the Deliveroo drivers
who are actually
turning now to cheer

up pops the pram cover
the incredulous look
and you're laughing now
the wind in your hair   *you fabulous bitch*
and then you

bounce   into the road   and up the other side

million-dollar smile for the crowd   they love you
and above you the full Red Arrow treatment as
you execute a flawless brake   bellowing   *not out loud obviously*
we are going to make it
        we are going to fucking make it!

In the lily room

In the lily room we are learning
everything is both itself and the symbol of itself.

*

Lilies are to living
as rocks are to raccoons. Rock on!

We ask, where is the moon today.
Is it a lacquer tray or a thin, thin smile.

*

Some things are knowable – for the most part
the recycling truck comes on Tuesdays.

Clementines are crowned with stars.
See how the rain falls upwards on this strawberry.

*

We find we have it in us
to be as earnest as balcony sprigs.

*

A big thing, a medium thing
and a small thing makes a family.

For example saucepans.
For example acorns – beads – lint.

*

We remind each other of ourselves,
falling silent in the mirror.

*

In the lily room stickers are underfoot
and pencils are cracked all the way down.

Unpredictable surfaces.
A scrawl on the wall by the door –

siren blue for the day we left her to it
while we tore at each other with low voices.

*

We pick up the grains of rice one by one,
like astronauts.

After her bath she checks my hair for lions.
Dishes queue up by the sink.

*

We ask, what if the tomatoes stay green.
What if we got it wrong at the start.

But she knows the tins will right themselves
if we just turn back the page.

*

In the lily room time is a handspan,
a tangle of bright wool.

Watch out, Mr Clumsy!
we shout, warm and safe on the carpet

Compline

We will lay us down in peace

and I will press my nose into your back
until you turn over – a boulder –
and there will be a relenting behind your eyes
although it is over a year since we slept a full night
and we are skinless – blanched as stricken trees –
and some days I am terrified
it is already too late for us

but I will cover you like a pelt if you ask me to
and you will trace leafy shapes between my shoulder blades
and tomorrow I will be a mouse in your pocket
and you will be a blown egg in mine
and we will carry one another

and take our rest.

Morning

You kneel behind her
holding open the coat

all the coats
she's ever worn

watch her disappear
into the sleeves.

You reach over
to pull up the zip

the dome of her chattering head
against your chin

the smell of it
stopping time.

Her arms loop round
to claim yours

heavy and warm and real
squeezing tight

the safe crook
of your elbows.

You hold it
between you

this breath
this grief.

Duet

Now that we have it by heart

(milk on my lap, then onto the green chair –
a story, a song – milk again,
into the cot – one last story – just one more last one)

these days we delight
in sketching out the phrases,

gesturing nightly with the sweeping line
of an arm, the tilt of a chin

to those tender selves
who laid down the parts
in deadly earnest –

out of need, back then,
not yet as art

Song for my mother

青い青いお空です / What a blue blue sky
雲がポッカリ浮いていて / With fluffy clouds drifting
太陽ギラギラ照りつける / And the sun beaming bright
高い富士山も見てるだろう / I bet Mt Fuji is looking down too

Suddenly I see her, aged four. There is an alice band in her hair, a summer breeze, and as she pushes off with her red sandals the swing climbs higher, higher ~

A brand-new song. When her brother comes home she will sing it to him. From the highest point on the swing she can see Fuji-san, distant and familiar. All she wants in the world is to mean something to the people she loves, to be held tight and cherished.

Six decades later, her daughter and granddaughter are listening on FaceTime. It is morning where we are; there are porridge stains on our pyjamas and the puzzles are already out of their tin. Outside my mother's window the sky is dark as it always is. On a June day in our imaginations the brand-new song floats towards the clouds ~

What it takes for her to offer it to us, a century egg in its shell. She needs us to handle it with love, but we can't even open it at first – we don't speak her language. N's attention wanders; she knows this is important but she is very busy just now, writing her own story. As for me, the threads of my heart are stretching but there has been so much hurt, so much water. It is not easy to greet my mother as the child she once was.

That final line: was it だろう, confident, brash even, or was it かな, delicate and open-ended? She can't remember now which of these she used to be. We are trying to glimpse her through such a little window.

I prop the phone up against a book to improvise a circle. We point to the clouds, make sunbursts with our fingers, raise our arms to form the mountain above our heads. What else can we do but sing it over and over, until it becomes a part of us.

Lately her hand floats free of mine during feeds.
Still going after all this time! You deserve a cruise, mum—

I watch her moving further from me, my muse,
her steps sure through the lengthening grass. 'Mummy!'

Mummy: how precious now, that name,
in the mouth of a child full enough to choose.

In the green light of evening she returns, my baby.
No more forms to fill; we've paid our dues.

Last feed

the ferret-smell of her neck
the kitten-smell of her hair
the parsley-smell of her cheek

I feel my milk pull
down into the waiting ducts

an electric pulse
lighting up the sister moons
my deep-sleeping womb

this pleasure still foreign
hard-won

though the cracking spilling
bruising obsessing months are
fading now

our silence the silence
of animals concentrating

the weight of her body
her fists buried in
my stomach folds

the warm huff of her breath
the sweet insistence of her teeth

my soft flesh
held between her jaws
as if it were newborn

Balloons

In the video she is kicking balloons,
laughing and laughing as they
boing with abandon around the living room.

The evening after Daddy's birthday.
Later we'll tell stories in bed,
where all of the past counts as yesterday:

the time at the park she boffed her head
on the Big Slide, or the time we took
the train to Chinatown to visit the red

lanterns just like the ones in her book –
slumbering fishing boats lit by sunrise.
Yesterday we bought one for the hook

on her ceiling. It watched her memorise
all the numbers on her hopscotch rug;
tumble on her mattress like a pint-size

circus clown; mend her stuffed toys with hugs
(that's better); outgrow the orange shoes.
Tomorrow she will start to shrug

off our kisses – we have it all to lose –
but last night she ran in from a nightmare
and we slept as a pack, pressed close.

In the photo we don't have a care
in the world. We're sipping pretend tea
from real cups in our underwear

and feeling suddenly, scarily lucky.
Yesterday I was certain our world
was too fragile for three. But already I see

that the baby from the album is a girl.
Clutching her balloons she races
towards the lens – limbs unfurled,

triumphant in her weightlessness.

Epilogue

At the next table, a woman is speaking loudly to her friend.
'… I knew I was being difficult but mentally I couldn't stand

it a minute longer so I just discharged myself, my innards
were all out of place, it was so lonely at night on the ward…'

On and on with barely a breath. The diners around
her titter, rolling their eyes at how *insane* she sounds

with her torrent of detail, her reservoir of distress
disgorging onto the silent friend. Six weeks in, I would guess.

I pay attention to my response. No dull ache, no whiplash.
Now, I'm just another regular with a latte. I watch

the friend shifting in her seat – her own child waiting to ask
if he can have an ice cream – a pair of older women in masks

easing out of quilted coats – the waiter mopping up a spilled
vase of purple flowers – and marvel at life's forward tilt.

Hand-me-downs

Expectant mother.
Well-travelled pram with fresh wheels
bouncing down the street.

Bodysuits rolled like rosebuds –
a bundle taking up space.

Pigeons on the grass
underneath our balcony
strung with socks like charms.

I find myself beguiling
in this temporary dress.

Beautiful moon :
the sound of breathing… in… out…
a body working.

3am – dry leaves rustling,
her mew pulling like a tide.

Afternoon lamp light;
cat onesie with sleeves rolled up;
celebration arms.

It's all foxes or flowers
or rainbows or unicorns.

'I ♥ NYC' –
I know I should lighten up,
but she's never been.

Dungarees for next summer,
swapping notes on Sertraline.

Circle of mothers,
the truth ripe plums in our mouths.
Paying it forward.

I wasn't ready for this
salt on my baby's soft hair.

First trip to the sea,
dressed as a green dinosaur.
The sky is so vast…

In black and white pyjamas
she points to the moon, then Mars.

Now the days are short;
light slanting through the window;
dinner on the hob.

Mashed pear on her red shift dress,
another new favourite.

In the Future Bag
sensational floral-print
dresses are waiting.

We are filling up a box
for our friend's rainbow baby.

That swimming costume –
sailor stripes, frou-frou pink swan,
0-12 months size.

But you were just a marble
rolling around in my womb.

Not everyone lives.
A mournful theme echoing,
little clouds of breath.

> The task of not being crushed
> by grief; digging the new bed.

Wood anemone –
one, two, ten, exponential –
the start of something.

> The clocks go forward tonight;
> Googling herd immunity.

Blowing bubbles :
early summer in the park,
keeping our distance.

> The charity shop is closed.
> 'Please don't leave your bags outside.'

Changeable weather;
we'll pass on the brown bear coat
when it's safe to meet.

> Woodland walk in the splash suit,
> kicking up leaves with Daddy.

Her forest moon dress
was too big; now it's too small –
this keeps happening…

Stomping on the jungle gym.
Roooarrr! Godzilla with milk teeth.

Life's not a movie.
Pregnancy after stillbirth;
counting down the weeks.

We can't send them anything
until the baby makes it.

Words words words all day.
Everything has a colour;
the pine cones are green.

So much to be examined
in this metamorphosis.

Flamingo dress :
dancing in the living room,
never mind the rain.

New scooter – a blur of blue
in the wild flower meadow.

For Nicky, Gwen, Astrid, Nikki, Hollie, Louise and Helen

June

We left her jumper at the house
and now our daughter
is bare-armed
and slightly too cold
but my god
she is glorious
in her rainbow taffeta skirt,
flying her first ever kite
as if she's spent
a lifetime of unbroken summers
perfecting the art,
pulling the pale string
this way and that
like a partner at a dance,
its sun and moon faces
both beaming.
In the distance
Grandma waves from a bench,
impressed,
while at our daughter's feet
we, giddy parents,
lie back on wind-whipped grass,
hands shading our eyes,
marvelling
at the blue,
feeling festive and delicious
all of a sudden,
the tips of our fingers,
our hips, lifting
and later
we will touch each other

like teens
under the starched
spare-room duvet,
a late breeze
kissing
the curtain's edge and night
never falling

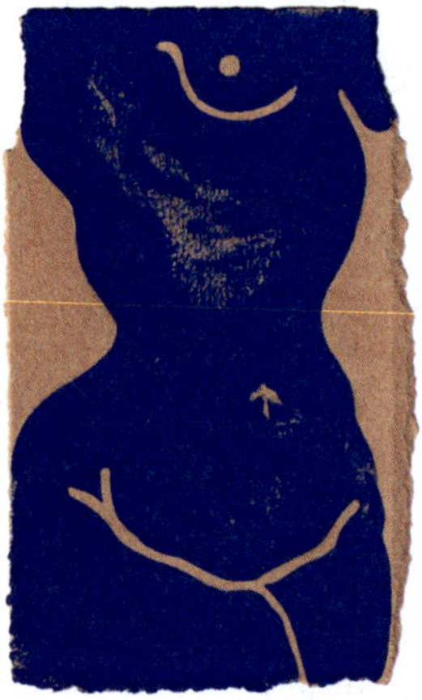

Notes

'Birth notes' and 'Hand-me-downs' are thirty-six-verse kasen renga chains, a form innovated and popularised by Matsuo Bashō. Kasen renga tends to incorporate elements such as a 5-7-5 / 7-7 syllabic structure, the use of seasonal words in every verse, and verses at specific points in the chain that refer to the moon or flowers. I have tried to honour these traditions in English, while taking some liberties with the form.

'Pigeon' was inspired by Emily Berry's poem 'Bird, Therapy, Fish Tank'.

'For the concerned spouse' was inspired by the story of Izanagi and Izanami, the central deities in the Japanese creation myth. Izanami famously dies in childbirth and descends to the underworld. I learned more recently that there is a (less popular) version of the myth in which Izanami doesn't die but rather lives a long and peaceful life.

'Compline': In the Christian tradition of canonical hours, the compline is the final prayer service of the day.

'In praise of Sertraline': Sertraline is a type of antidepressant known as a selective serotonin reuptake inhibitor (SSRI). It's commonly prescribed to treat depression and anxiety.

'South London air' uses a device I loved in Chrissy Williams's poem 'JON SPENCER BLUES EXPLOSION in the Spring'.

'Safety advice': On 16 March 2022, the Donetsk Regional Drama Theatre in Mariupol was bombed during the Russian invasion of Ukraine. Up to 1,300 civilians were reportedly sheltering in the basement of the theatre in the days before 16 March when the city was under siege.

'The fish' is based on 'The Fish' by Elizabeth Bishop.

‘Live action role-play’: Live action role-play, or LARP, is a form of role-playing game where the participants pursue goals within a fictional setting represented by real-world environments, whilst interacting with each other in character. The setting and rules for the game are determined by the arrangers of the game, who are called ‘gamemasters’.

‘Sleep songs’: This poem started out as a golden shovel, based on three children’s songs taught to me by the musician Oren Marshall – ‘When we wake up’, ‘The moon is dancing in the treetops’ and ‘I like to bounce’. The lyrics are still nestled in the final poem, but not always used as end-words.

‘In the lily room’ was inspired by Laura Wittner’s poem ‘Dentro de casa’ (‘Inside the house’).

‘Song for my mother’: ‘…だろう’ roughly translates as ‘I bet…’, while ‘…かな’ translates as ‘I wonder if…’

*

If you or someone you know is suffering with postpartum mental ill-health, the below organisations offer support and advice in the UK:

- Maternal Mental Health Alliance (maternalmentalhealthalliance.org)
- Association for Post Natal Illness (apni.org)
- Tommy’s: The Pregnancy and Baby Charity (tommys.org)
- Mind (mind.org.uk)
- NHS Talking Therapies (www.england.nhs.uk/mental-health/adults/nhs-talking-therapies/)

Acknowledgements

Thank you to Jane and Angela at Nine Arches Press for believing in this book, for taking such care over its production and for helping it to reach people.

Thank you to Laxmi Hussain for the beautiful cover art.

Thank you to Clare Pollard, Liz Berry and Nora Thurkle for advice on early drafts of the manuscript.

Thank you to the following magazines, journals and zines where some of the poems first appeared: *Ink Sweat & Tears, Choices* (Mum Poem Press), *The North, Propel, Lunate, The Friday Poem, And Other Poems, Basket, Strix Leeds, PERVERSE, Magma, Acumen, Under the Radar, harana poetry, London Grip, The Idler, The High Window* and *Motherlore Magazine*.

'Tidings' won second prize in the 2022 Winchester Poetry Prize. 'Water music' was commended in the 2023 Stanza Poetry Competition. 'Night feed' was commended in the 2023 Magma Poetry Competition (Editors' Prize). 'In the lily room' was longlisted in the 2023 National Poetry Competition. 'South London air' was shortlisted for the 2025 Free Verse Prize.

Thank you to the poets who have taught me (so far): Liz Berry, Peter Sansom, Jen Hadfield, Wendy Pratt, Arji Manuelpillai, Kat Lyons, Kim Moore, Jonathan Edwards, Clare Shaw, Pascale Petit, Will Harris, Vanessa Kisuule and Katrina Naomi.

Thank you to my poetry families: the JAM, the Steamies, the Lyric Selves, the Form Fillers and the Linenists.

Thank you to my friends at the Poetry Translation Centre.

Thank you to Anna Selby, Chris McCabe, Laura Sampson, Nina Segal, Alison Beck, Georgia Rodger, Alison Winter, Alissa Figueirado, Octavia Lamb, Chrissy Williams, Leo Boix, Sophie Ransby, Jacqui Nix, Sophie Heavey, Alice Wightwick, Frances Hatherley, Tia Gatley, Emma Jackson, Helen Morris, Nichola Smalley, Kirsten Scott and Katie Maguire.

Thank you to my mother – 大好き.

Finally, thank you to G and N – this book is dedicated to you.